YOUR KNOWLEDGE HAS VALUE

- We will publish your bachelor's and master's thesis, essays and papers

- Your own eBook and book - sold worldwide in all relevant shops

- Earn money with each sale

Upload your text at www.GRIN.com
and publish for free

Alexander Eriksröd

A Doubtful Contribution. Review of Anthony Carty: "The Iraq Invasion as a Recent United Kingdom 'Contribution' to International Law"

GRIN Publishing

Bibliographic information published by the German National Library:

The German National Library lists this publication in the National Bibliography; detailed bibliographic data are available on the Internet at http://dnb.dnb.de .

Imprint:

Copyright © 2014 GRIN Verlag GmbH
Print and binding: Books on Demand GmbH, Norderstedt Germany
ISBN: 978-3-656-86292-5

This book at GRIN:

http://www.grin.com/en/e-book/285981/a-doubtful-contribution-review-of-anthony-carty-the-iraq-invasion-as

GRIN - Your knowledge has value

Since its foundation in 1998, GRIN has specialized in publishing academic texts by students, college teachers and other academics as e-book and printed book. The website www.grin.com is an ideal platform for presenting term papers, final papers, scientific essays, dissertations and specialist books.

Visit us on the internet:

http://www.grin.com/

http://www.facebook.com/grincom

http://www.twitter.com/grin_com

A Doubtful Contribution

Review of Anthony Carty: "The Iraq Invasion as a Recent United Kingdom
'Contribution' to International Law"

Alexander Martin Eriksroed

October 2014

—

The Basics of International Law & Issues of International Law and War

—

Année universitaire 2014/2015
Collège universitaire / Campus de Nancy
Semestre d'automne

TABLE OF CONTENTS

A DOUBTFUL CONTRIBUTION

CONTENT OUTLINE

In „The Iraq Invasion as a Recent United Kingdom 'Contribution to International Law'", published in the *European Journal of International Law* Vol. 16 no. 1 in 2005, Anthony Carty argues that the United Kingdom (hereafter UK), through its participation in the Iraq invasion and war of 2003 has set a precedent for pre-emptive attacks in international law (hereafter referred to as IL). The legal scholar and professor at Hong Kong University and Aberdeen University questions the legality of the use of force by the UK and United States of America (hereafter US) and legitimacy of the regime change that followed. Carty also discusses the influence of advisors on high-level political decision-making, as in the case of Robert Cooper affecting Tony Blair.[1]

This abstract gives an overview of the article's main ideas and historical and political context such as how Britain (together with its allies) framed Saddam Hussein as a threat to international peace in order to build up support for its intervention. It focusses thereafter on linking the events of 2003 to a new notion of and dramatic changes within IL and the question of what actions of foreign policy are internationally (generally) acceptable as a result of the Iraq invasion.

---

[1] Eriksroed, Alexander, "A doubtful contribution". Review of *Anthony Carty's "The Iraq Invasion as a recent United Kingdom Contribution to International Law". The European Journal of International Law* 16 no. 1 (2005): 143-151.

BACKGROUND SYNOPSIS

In the mornings of March 20, 2003, the US led the so-called 'coalition of the willing' (US, UK, Australia, Poland and Peshmerga [armed Kurdish fighters]) into Iraq in a military operation entitled 'Operation Iraqi Liberation' (later changed to 'Operation Iraqi Freedom'). There had neither been an official declaration of war nor (unanimous) consent about the way the US and UK justified and sought to legitimize their going to war.[2] [3]

THE DOUBTFUL 'CONTRIBUTION' TO IL

In three propositions, Carty brings forward the UK's questionable contribution to the development of IL.

Firstly, by invading a sovereign state, which had not directly threatened the invading force, the UK set a precedent for pre-emptive attacks in IL.[4] What legally justified the invasion, in the eyes of the UK, was that the Iraqi regime under Saddam Hussein posed a serious threat as it might use or pass on weapons of mass destruction (hereafter referred to as WMD) to terrorist groups in Iraq and neighboring states.[5] To be exact, Iraq's "non-compliance" with paragraph 3 and 4 of the United Nations Security Council (hereafter: UN-SC) resolution 1441 was cited. The responsibility to protect the people of Iraq from the Saddam regime was also mentioned, although to a far lesser extent.[6]

Secondly, Carty argues (rightly so) that, by ignoring the UN Charter's prohibition of the use of force in article 2(4), the UK rejected the authority of the UN-SC and IL altogether.

Thirdly, the Iraq invasion of 2003 was the first time that invading forces had openly and publicly stated regime change as a legally permissible objective. It was

---

[2] El-Shibiny, Mohamed, "Iraq: A Lost War" (2010).
[3] Sharma, S.R., "US-Iraq War: an Erosion of UN Authority" (2003), 152-174.
[4] Dixon, Martin, „Textbook on International Law" (2013), 142-171.
[5] Sharma, 47-56.
[6] "Council on Foreign Relations: IRAQ: Justifying the War":
http://www.cfr.org/iraq/iraq-justifying-war/p7689#p0 (Accessed on October 6, 2014)

US Army General Tommy Franks who stated that the objective was "[...] to end the regime of Saddam Hussein".[7]

INFLUENCE OF ADVISORS ON POLITICAL DECISION-MAKING

Carty develops the argument that the influence of political counselors, who have direct access to senior policy officials, is not to be underestimated in analyzing the reasons for and effects of political decision-making. He presents the example of British strategist Robert Cooper, one of then-UK Prime Minister Tony Blair's closest advisors on the Iraq war. In his well-known text "The Breaking of Nations" (2003), Cooper formulates a general principle which is incompatible with IL as laid out in the UN Charter. In his three categories into which he divides the international society (*pre-modern, modern* and *post-modern states)*, Cooper places the UN in the modern sphere. He classifies, in his work "The Post-Modern State and the World Order" (2000) the so-called *failed states* as pre-modern. He agrees with Max Weber in referring to *failed states* as nations in which the state no longer has the legitimate monopoly on the use of force.[8] Cooper continues by addressing the incompatibility between his three state categories. The language of the UN, he argues, does not apply to *failed states* in the *pre-modern* category. For the UK government, this served as the basis of their interpretation of the non-application of the 'UN sphere' and its regulations, constituting another facet of the justification for going to war.

Carty goes on to discuss how Cooper believes that IL is obsolete in a world in which force is the ultimate guarantor of security, most notably in a world of nuclear anarchy, in which self-defense will be too late, thus taking a stance for pre-emptive strikes. Furthermore, Cooper argues that it would be irresponsible to let even one further country acquire nuclear (or other WMD) capabilities. Arguably, both of these notions played into the UK's decision to join the US in invading Iraq.

AUTHOR'S COMMENTS

[7] "New York Times Learning Network: Missions Accomplished?":
http://learning.blogs.nytimes.com/2003/04/11/missions-accomplished/?_php=true&_type=blogs&_r=0 (Accessed on October 5, 2014)
[8] Cooper, Robert, "The Post-Modern State and the World Order" (2000), 15.

After this outline of Carty's main opinions on the Iraq invasion in terms of IL, I shall now expand his thinking by elaborating on some of my own thoughts.

The UK's 'contribution' to IL, as Carty so aptly puts it, is rather doubtful as it neither respects current IL regimes nor attempts to improve on them. In my view, states' non-respect of IL regimes (to which they have officially adhered in most cases – that is to say which they demand other states adhere to) can only be justified in the case of 'over-fulfillment' (applying stricter rules to oneself than legally necessary). This situation, clearly, does not apply. The UK simply went (together with the US, that is) its own way, putting itself above generally accepted regulations of IL by - seeing it positively, applying a rather questionable interpretation of - or, seeing it negatively, altogether ignoring - the verdict of the UN-SC. Kofi Annan, former UNSG reiterated time and time again, last in September 2014, that from the point of view of the UN Charter the war was illegal, basing his verdict on Art. 39 of the UN Charter which gives the UN-SC the right to rule on the legality of war.[9]

What makes this violation of IL so outrageous is the fact that it concerns the most basic questions of statehood and international security. If even the territorial sovereignty of other states (hence the most fundamental part of the UN Charter[10]) are questioned, doors to doubting many other, much more intricate and delicate basic assumptions of IL are opened. This precisely illustrates the dilemma of non-enforceability of IL and the reliance on the willingness of states to adhere to regulations commonly agreed on, constituting a main differentiation to law as known in the domestic sphere.

Former US President G.W Bush even argued, in his speech to the UN General Assembly on September 12, 2002, that the UN-SC was obliged to act both from a moral standpoint and from a standpoint of self-interest; otherwise it would never again be taken seriously. This demonstrates how great powers (or their allies) can get away with violations of even the most fundamental and most widely acknowledged basis of IL: state sovereignty.

---

[9] "Iraq war was illegal and breached UN Charter, says Annan"
http://www.theguardian.com/world/2004/sep/16/iraq.iraq (Accessed on October 16, 2014)
[10] Article 2(4), Charter of the United Nations

Equally worrying is the fact that in justifying the war, 'higher moral obligations' were once again cited – providing a welcome argument for politicians. I do not draw the general moral obligation of fighting against proliferation of WMD in order to "make the world a safer place" into doubt. Neither do I question that there is some genuine truth behind Bush or Blair wanting to protect the world from WMD being employed. What is appalling though, is how – in a Bismarckian fashion of Realpolitik – certain states compromise the territorial integrity of other states without blinking an eye while, at the same time, demanding of others to adhere to regulations of IL. Ultimately, state leaders must either adopt Cooper's (or even more incisive: Mearsheimer's) understanding of ultimate anarchy and be frank about it or, on the contrary, view (and support) IL as an attempt to somewhat structure an unstable and often disconcerting world. With this issue, compromise is just not to be brought about. Today's situation of Iraq and the Middle East region is a stark reminder.

BIBLIOGRAPHY

Literature

- Dixon, Martin. "Textbook on International Law" (2013).

- Al-Shibiny, Mohamed. "Iraq: A Lost War" (2010).

- Sharma, S.R. "US-Iraq War: an Erosion of UN Authority" (2003).

- Cooper, Robert. "The Post-Modern State and the World Order" (2000).

Online sources

- Pan, Esther. Council on Foreign Relations. "IRAQ: Justifying the War"
  http://www.cfr.org/iraq/iraq-justifying-war/p7689#p0
  (October 6, 2014)

- Sale, Michelle and Khan, Javaid. New York Times. "Learning Network:
  Missions Accomplished?"
  http://learning.blogs.nytimes.com/2003/04/11/missions-
  accomplished/?_php=true&_type=blogs&_r=0
  (October 5, 2014)

- MacAscill Ewen and Borger Julian. The Guardian. "Iraq war was illegal and
  breached UN Charter, says Annan"
  http://www.theguardian.com/world/2004/sep/16/iraq.iraq
  (October 6, 2014)